Publishing

www.spinereaders.com

Copyright © JD S'more 2024
All rights reserved.

This book or any portion thereof may not be reproduced or used in any manner whatsoever without the written permission of the publisher except for the use of brief quotations in a book review.

Notes for Adults

This book can be used as a tool to help children identify and manage their emotions in a fun and positive way.

Being able to recognize emotions is important for the development and mental well-being in people of all ages. Learning how to express your feelings can help people understand more about themselves and the world around them. Some find this harder than others, and that is completely Okay. Always encourage them with kindness.

Use the activities and games at the end of this book to help grow their confidence and knowledge while learning at their own pace in a safe environment.

Charlies Ninja Day

Written by J.D. S'more
Illustrated by Tim Bye

My name is Charlie
and later I have ninja class.

I'm so EXCITED!
I can't figure out how to make
the time pass.

I feel a bit **IMPATIENT** like I don't want to wait. I just want to get there and not worry about being late.

I put on my clothes and get myself ready.

I try to stay CALM and keep myself steady.

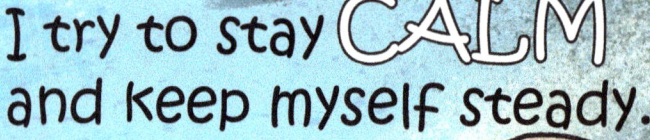

This waiting game is hard,
but it's what I must do.

I stop for a second and think,
"UM.... NO!".

I start to get FLUSTERED
"Where could my shoe be?"
and in that moment,
I get down on my knee.

Ah ha! There it is right under my bag.
If I didn't find it, that would have been a drag.

I put on my shoe and in a flash I'm outside,

On the drive over we get stuck behind cars.
"This is so long! Are we driving to mars?"

He laughs at me when I try my best. It makes me feel like I'm not as good as the rest.

Ari swings on the rings and does very good.

When I hop on the rings, I try my best like I should.

Teddy says something rude like I knew that he would.

I finished them all like I knew that I could!

I'm in charge of my feelings,
so here's what I learned today,
There is no need to listen
to what rude people say!

Ari and I finished the day
with a great big...

Finish the Picture

What emotion do you think Charlie is feeling? Draw the face to match the emotion!

The emotion I have drawn is:
_____

Mix & Match Game

With the help of an adult, cut out these cards then turn them all over so you can't see them and lay them out on a flat surface.

Take turns flipping any two cards over. If the emotions match, you keep them and try again. If they don't match, it is the next person's turn.

After all the cards have gone, the winner is the player with the most emotions. Good luck!

Mix Up

Can you unscramble the letters to create an emotion?
(Answers on the bottom of the page - no peeking!)

WORELFUP _ _ _ _ _ _ _

DAS _ _ _ _ _ _ _ _ _ _ _ _

TRONGS _ _ _ _ _ _ _ _ _

GRAYN _ _ _ _ _ _ _ _ _ _

PAPHY _ _ _ _ _ _ _ _ _ _

ANSWERS = POWERFUL, SAD, STRONG, ANGRY, HAPPY

Spot the Difference

Can you find the 5 differences between these 2 pictures?

Questions & Answers

1. What is something that makes you feel excited?

----

2. Can you think of a time that made you feel impatient?

----

3. What does happiness feel like?

----

4. How do you think Charlie was feeling when he first saw Teddy?

----

5. Do you have a friend like Ari? Why do you think friends are important?

----

6. When were you most proud of yourself? What was it for?

About the Author

J.D S'more is the mother of five beautiful children in the USA.

Spreading Happiness is her second book inspired by her daughter and aimed to introduce young children to emotions in a fun and unique way.

J.D. S'more has written more books in the series and plans to expand her brand into accompanying products. Find out more at spinereaders.com

www.ingramcontent.com/pod-product-compliance
Lightning Source LLC
Chambersburg PA
CBHW041153110526
44590CB00027B/4223